A Chapter in the Philosophy of Value

Georg Simmel

A Chapter in the Philosophy of Value

Georg Simmel

American Journal of Sociology, vol. 5, 1900

The fact of economic exchange confers upon the value of things something super-individual. It detaches them from dissolution in the mere subjectivity of the agents, and causes them to determine each other reciprocally, since each exerts its economic function in the other. The practically effective value is conferred upon the object, not merely by its own desirability, but by the desirability of another object. Not merely the relationship to the receptive subjects characterizes this value, but also the fact that it arrives at this relationship only at the price of a sacrifice; while from the opposite point of view this sacrifice appears as a good to be enjoyed, and the object in question, on the contrary, as a sacrifice. Hence the objects acquire a reciprocity of counterweight, which makes value appear in a quite special manner as an objective quality indwelling in themselves. While the object itself is the thing in controversy

-- which means that the sacrifice which it represents is being determined -- its significance for both contracting parties appears much more as something outside of these latter and self-existent than if the individual thought of it only in its relation to himself. We shall see later how also isolated industry, by placing the workman over against the demands of nature, imposes upon him the like necessity of sacrifice for gaining of the object, so that in this case also the like relationship, with the one exception that only a single party has been changed, may endow the object with the same independent qualities, yet with their significance dependent upon its own objective conditions. Desire and the feeling of the agent stand, to be sure, as the motor energy behind all this, but from this in and of itself this value form could not proceed. It rather comes only from the reciprocal counterbalancing of the objects.

To be sure, in order that equivalence and exchange of values may emerge, some material to which value can attach must be at the basis. For industry as such the fact that these materials are equivalent to each other and exchangeable is the turning-point.

It guides the stream of appraisal through the form of exchange, at the same time creating a middle realm between desires, in which all human movement has its source, and the satisfaction of enjoyment in which it culminates. The specific character of economic activity as a special form of commerce exists, if we may venture the paradox, not so much in the fact that it exchanges values as that it exchanges values. To be sure, the significance which things gain in and with exchange rests never isolated by the side of their subjective-immediate significance, that is, the one originally decisive of the relationship. It is rather the case that the two belong together, as form and content connote each other. But the Objective procedure makes an abstraction, so to speak, from the fact that values constitute its material, and derives its peculiar character from the equality of the same --

somewhat as geometry finds its tasks only in connection with the magnitude -- relations of things, without bringing into its consideration the substances in connection with which alone these relationships actually have existence. That thus not only reflection upon industry, but industry itself, consists, so to speak, in a real abstraction from the surrounding actuality of the appraising processes is not so wonderful as it at first appears when we once make clear to ourselves how extensively human practice, cognition included, reckons with abstractions.

The energies, relationships, qualities of things -- to which in so far our own proper essence also belongs_constitute objectively a unified interrelationship, which is divided into a multiplicity of independent series or motives only after the interposition of our interests, and in order to be manipulated by us. Accordingly, each science investigates phenomena which possess an exclusive unity, and clean-cut lines of division from the problems of other sciences, only from the point of view which the special science proposes as its own. Reality, on the other hand, has no regard to these boundary lines, but every section of the world presents a conglomeration of tasks for the most numerous sciences. Likewise our practice dissects from the external or internal complexity of things one-sided series. Notice, for example, into how many systems a forest is divided. These in turn become objects of special interest to a hunter, a proprietor, a poet, a painter, a civic official, a botanist, and a tourist. The forest is objectively always the same. It is a real, indivisible unity of al the determinations and relationships out of which the interested parties select each a certain group, and make it into a picture of the forest. The same is the case with the great systems of interest of which a civilization is composed. We distinguish, for instance, interests and relationships as the ethical, the egoistic, the economic, the domestic, etc. The reciprocal weaving together of these constitutes actual life.

Certain of these, however, dissociated from this concrete reality, constitute the content of the civic structure. The state is an abstraction of energies and reciprocal actions which, in the concrete, exist only within a unity that is not separable into its parts. Again, in like manner, pedagogy abstracts from the web of cosmic contents into the totality of which the pupil is subsequently to enter certain ones, and forms them into a world which is completely abstract, in comparison with reality.

In this world the pupil is to live. To what extent all art runs a

'division line of its own through the conditions of things, in addition to those that are traced out in the real structure of the objective world, needs no elaboration. In opposition to that naturalism which wanted to lead art away from the selective abstraction, and to open to it the whole breadth and unity of reality, in which all elements have equally rights, in so far as they are actual-precisely in opposition to this has criticism shown the complete impracticability of the tendency,. and that even the extremest purpose, to be satisfied in art only with undifferentiated completeness of the object, must at last end in an abstraction. It will merely be the product of another selective. principle. Accordingly,. this is one of the formulas in which we may express the relation of man to the world, viz., from the unity and the interpenetration of things in which each bears the other and all have equal rights our practice not less than our theory constantly abstracts isolated elements, and forms them into unities relatively complete in themselves. Except in quite general feelings, we have no relationship to the totality of being. Only when in obedience to the necessities of our thought and action we derive perpetual abstractions from phenomena, and endow these with the relative independence of a merely subjective coherence to which the continuity of the world-movement as objective gives no room, do we reach a relationship to the. world that is definite in its details.

Indeed, we may adopt a scale of values for our culture systems, according to the degree in which they combine the demands of our singular purposes with the possibility of passing over without a gap from each abstraction which they present to the other, so that a subsequent combination is possible which approximates that objective coherence and unity. Accordingly, the economic system of the world is assuredly founded upon an abstraction, that is, upon the relation of reciprocity and exchange, the balance between sacrifice and gain; while in the actual process in which this takes place it is inseparably amalgamated with its foundations and its results, the desires and the satisfactions.

But this form of existence does not distinguish it from the other territories into which, for the purposes of our interests, we subdivide the totality of phenomena.

The objectivity of economic value which we assume as defining the scope of economics, and which is thought as the independent characteristic of the same in distinction from its subjective vehicles and consequences, consists in its being true of many, or rather all, subjects. The decisive factor is its extension in principle beyond the individual. The fact that for one object another must be given shows that not merely for me, but also for itself, that is, also for another person, the object is of some value. The appraisal takes place in the form of economic value.

The exchange of objects, moreover,. in which this

objectivication, and therewith the specific character of economic activity, realizes itself belongs, from the standpoint of each of the contracting parties, in the quite general category of gain and loss, purpose and means. If any object over which we have control is to help us to the possession or enjoyment of another, it is generally under the condition that we forego the enjoyment of its own peculiar worth. As a rule the purpose consumes either the substance or the force of the means, so that the value of the same constitutes the price which must be paid for the value of the purpose. Only within certain spiritual interests is that not the case as a rule. The mind has been properly compared to a fire, in which countless candles may be lighted without loss of its own peculiar intensity. For example, intellectual products sometimes (not always) retain for purposes of instruction their own worth, which does not lose any of its independent energy and significance by functioning as means to the pedagogical end. In the case of causal series in external nature, however, the relationship is usually different. Here must the object, if on the one hand it is conceived immediately as valuable, and on the other hand as means to the attainment of another value, be sacrificed as a value in itself, in order to perform its office as means. This procedure rules all values the enjoyment of which is connected with a conscious action on our part. What we call exchange is obviously nothing but a special case of this typical form in human life. We must regard this, however, not merely as a placing of exchange in the universal category of creation of value; but, conversely, this latter as an exchange in the wider sense of the word. This possibility, which has so many consequences for the theory of value, will become clear by the discussion of the doctrine that all economic value consists in exchange value.

To this theory the objection has been made that even the quite isolated economic man -- he who neither sells nor buys --

must estimate his products and means of production according to their value, if expenditures and results are to stand in proper relation to each other. This objection, however, is not so striking as it appears, for all consideration whether a definite product is worth enough to justify a definite expenditure of labor or other goods is, for the economic agent, precisely the same as the appraisal which takes place in connection with exchange. In confronting the concept,, exchange,, there is frequently the confusion of ideas which consists in speaking of a relationship as though it were something apart from the elements between which it plays. It means, however, only a condition or a change within each of these elements, but nothing that is between them in the sense of a spatial object that can be distinguished in space between two other objects. When we compose the two acts or changes of condition which in reality take place into the notion "exchange," the conception is attractive that something has happened in addition to or beyond that which took place in each of the contracting parties. Considered with reference to its immediate content, exchange is nothing but the twofold repetition of the fact that an actor now has something which he previously did not have, and on the other hand does not have something which he previously had. That being the case, the isolated economic man, who surely must make a sacrifice to gain certain products, acts precisely like the one who makes exchanges. The only difference is that the party with whom he contracts is not a second sentient being, but the natural order and regularity of things, which no more satisfy our desires without a sacrifice on our part than would another person. His appraisals of value, in accordance with which he governs his actions, are, as a rule, precisely the same as in the case of exchange; for the economic actor, as such, it is surely quite immaterial whether the substances or labor-energies in his possession are sunk in the ground or given to another man, if only there accrues to him the same result from the sacrifice. This subjective process of sacrifice and gain in the individual soul is by no means something secondary or imitative in comparison with

inter-individual exchange; on the contrary, the give-and-take between sacrifice and accomplishment, within the individual, is the basal presumption, and at the same time the persistent substance, of every two-sided exchange. The latter is merely a sub-species of the former; that is, the sort in which the sacrifice is occasioned by the demand of another individual. At the same time, it can only be occasioned by the same sort of result for the actor so far as objects and their qualities are concerned. It is of extreme importance to make this reduction of the economic process to that which actually takes place, that is, in the soul of every economic agent. We must not allow ourselves to be deceived about the essential thing by the fact that in the case of exchange this process is reciprocal; that is, that it is conditioned by the like procedure in another. The main thing is that the natural and solitary economic transaction, if we may conceive of such a thing, runs back to the same fundamental form as two-sided exchange: to the process of equalization between two subjective occurrences within the individual. This is in its proper essence not affected by the secondary question whether the impulse to the process proceeds from the nature of things or the nature of man; whether it is a matter of purely natural economy or of exchange economy. All feelings of value, in other words, which are set free by producible objects are in general to be gained only by foregoing other values. At the same time, such sacrifice may consist, not only in that mediate labor for ourselves which appears as labor for others, but frequently enough in that quite immediate labor for our own personal purposes.

Moreover, those theories of value which discover in labor the absolute element of value accommodate themselves to this form of conception as to the higher and more abstract idea. Whoever labors sacrifices something which he possesses -- his labor-power, or his leisure, or his pleasure merely in the self-satisfying play of his powers -- in order to get in exchange for these something which he does not possess. Through the fact that labor accomplishes this it acquires value, just as, on the other side, the attained object is valuable for the reason that it has cost labor. In so far there is not the slightest ground to give labor a special position as contrasted with all other conditions of value. The difference between these is only of a quantitative nature. Labor is the most frequent object of exchange.

In this assertion we forbear to enter into the discussion whether labor or labor-power, and in what form, constitute an object of exchange. Because labor is regarded as a sacrifice, as something painful, it is performed only when an object can be secured by it which corresponds to the

eudaemonistic or some other demand. If labor were nothing but pleasure, the products that it wrings from nature would have no value whatever, provided we disregard the difference in abundance of objects. On the contrary, if objects that satisfy our desires came to us of their own accord, labor would have no more value.

Thus on the whole we may say that, considered from the standpoint of value, every economic transaction is an exchange, and every single article of value furnishes its additional quota to the total value of life only after deduction of a certain sacrificed quantum of value.

In all the foregoing it is presupposed that a definite scale of value exists in the case of the objects, and that each of the two objects concerned in the transaction signifies, for the one contracting party the desired gain, for the other the necessary sacrifice. But this presumption is, as a matter of fact, much too simple. If, as is necessary, we regard economic activity as a special case of the universal life-form of exchange, as a sacrifice in return for a gain, we shall from the beginning suspect something of what takes place within this form, namely, that the value of the gain is not, so to speak, brought with it, ready-made, but it accrues to the desired object, in part or even entirely, through the measure of the sacrifice demanded in acquiring it. These cases, which are as frequent as they are important for the theory of value, seem, to be sure, to harbor an essential contradiction; for they require us to make a sacrifice of value for things which in themselves are worthless. As a matter of course, no one would forego value without receiving for it at least equal value; and, on the contrary, that the end should receive its value only through the price that we must give for it could be the case only in a crazy world. This is now, for immediate consciousness, correct. Indeed, it is more correct than that popular standpoint is apt to allow in other cases. As a matter of fact, the value which an actor surrenders for another value can never be greater for this actor himself, under the actual circumstances of the moment, than the one for which it is given. All contrary appearances rest upon confusion of the value actually estimated by the actor with the value which the object of exchange in question usually has. For instance, when one at the point of death from hunger offers a jewel for a piece of bread, he does it only because the latter, under the given circumstances, is of more value to him than the former.

Particular circumstances, however, are necessary in order to attach to an object a valuation, for every such valuation is an incident of the whole complex system of our. feelings, which is in constant flux, adaptation, and reconstruction. Whether these circumstances are exceptional or relatively constant is obviously in principle a matter of indifference. There can be no doubt, at any rate, that in the moment of the exchange, that is, of the making of the sacrifice, the value of the exchanged object forms the limit which is the highest point to which the value of the sacrificed object can rise. Quite independent of this is the question whence that former object derives its so necessary value, and whether it may come from the objects that are to be sacrificed for it, so that the equivalence between gain and price would be established at once a posteriori, and by the latter. We shall see presently how often value comes into existence, psychologically, in this apparently illogical manner. If, however, it is once in existence, the psychological necessity exists in its case, not less than in that of value constituted in any other way, of regarding it as a positive good at least equal to the negative good sacrificed for it. In fact, there is a series of cases in which the sacrifice not merely raises the value of the aim, but even produces it. It is the joy of exertion, of overcoming difficulties, frequently indeed that of contradiction, which expresses itself in this process. The necessary detour to the attainment of certain things is often the occasion, often also the cause, of regarding them as valuable. In the relationships of men to each other, most frequently and evidently in erotic relations, we notice how reserve, indifference, or repulse inflames the most passionate desire to conquer in spite of these obstacles, and spurs us to efforts and sacrifices which, without these obstacles, would surely seem to us excessive. For many people the aesthetic results of ascending the high Alps would not be considered worth further notice, if it did not demand extraordinary effort and danger, and if it did not thereby acquire tone, attractiveness, and consecration. The charm of antiquities and curiosities is frequently no other. If no sort of aesthetic or historical interest attaches to them, a substitute for it is furnished by the mere difficulty of acquiring them. They are worth just what they cost. This, then, appears secondarily to mean that they cost what they are worth.

Furthermore, all moral merit signifies that for the sake of the morally desirable deed contrary impulses and wishes must be fought down and sacrificed. If the act occurs without any conquest, as the matter-of-course outflow of unrestrained impulse, it is not appraised so high in the scale of subjective moral value, however desirable objectively its content may be. In this latter case we are not moral in any other sense than the flower is beautiful; we do not reckon the beauty of the flower as an ethical merit. Only through the sacrifice of the lower and still.so seductive good is the height of moral merit attained, and a more lofty height, the more attractive the temptation and the deeper and more comprehensive the sacrifice. We might array illustrations, beginning with the ordinary selfishness of the day, the overcoming of which alone rewards us with.the consciousness of being somewhat worthy, and rising to that force of logic whose sacrifice in favor of belief in the absurd seemed to the schoolmen an extreme religious merit. If we observe which human achievements attain to the highest honors and appraisals, we find it to be always those which betray a maximum of humility, effort, persistent concentration of the whole being, or at least seem to betray these. In other words, they seem to manifest the most self-denial, sacrifice of all that is subsidiary, and of devotion of the subjective to the objective ideal. And if, in contrast with all this, aesthetic production and everything easy, inviting, springing from the naturalness of impulse, unfolds an incomparable charm, this owes its special quality still to the undefined feeling of the burdens and sacrifices which are usually the condition of gaining such things. The mobility and inexhaustible power of combination of our mental content frequently brings it about that the significance of a correlation is carried over to its direct converse, somewhat as the association between two ideas occurs equally when they are asserted or denied of each other. The specific value of anything which we gain without conquered difficulty and as the gift of fortunate accident is felt by us only on the ground of the significance which the things have for us that are gained with difficulty and measured by sacrifice. It is the same value, but with the negative sign, and this is the primary from which the other may be derived; but the reverse is not the case.

If we look for an occurrence of this relationship within the economic realm, it seems to be demanded, in the first place, that we shall in thought separate the economic element, as a specific difference or form, from the fact of value as the universality or the substance of the same. If for the present we take value as a datum, and not now to be discussed, it is at least, in accordance with all the foregoing, not doubtful that economic value as such does not accrue to an object in its isolated self-existence, but only through the employment of another object which is given for it. Wild fruit picked without effort, and not given in exchange, but immediately consumed, is no economic good. It can count as such only when its consumption saves some other sort of economic expense. If, however, all the demands of life were to be satisfied in this fashion, so that no sacrifice was at any point necessary, men would simply not engage in industry, any more than do the birds or the fishes, or the denizens of fairy-land.

Whatever be the way in which the two objects, A and B, came to have value, A came to have an. economic value only through the fact that I must give B for it, B only through the fact that I can receive A for it. In this case, as above stated, it is in principle indifferent whether the sacrifice takes place by means of the transfer of a thing of value to another person, that is, through inter-individual exchange, or within the circle of the individual's own interests, through a balancing of efforts and results. In the articles of commerce there is nothing to be found but the significance which each has, directly or indirectly, for our need to consume, and the give-and-take that occurs between them. Since, now, as we have seen, the former does not of itself suffice to make the given object an object of economic activity, it follows that the latter alone can supply to it the specific difference which we call economic.

If thus, under the preliminary assumption of an existing value, the economic character of the same coincides with the offer of another object for it, and of it for the other object, there arises the further question whether this separation between the value and its economic form is necessary and possible. As a matter of fact, this artificially dividing abstraction finds in reality no counterpart. In the economic value the economic is as little sundered from the value as in the economic man the economist is sundered from the man. To be sure, man is possible in times and relations in which he does not pursue economic activity. The latter, however, is not possible without being accomplished by men, in absolute unity with them, and only in unreal conceptual abstraction is it to be sundered from them.

Thus there are enough objects of value which are not economic, but there are no objects of economic value which are not also valuable in every relation in which they are economic. What is true of the industry, as economic as such is, therefore, true of the values of every condition or quality or function is necessarily a condition or quality or function of that general object to which this quality or function pertains. The economic form of the value stands between two boundaries: on the one hand, the desire for the object, which attaches itself to the anticipated feeling of satisfaction from its possession and enjoyment; on the other hand, to this enjoyment itself, which, exactly considered, is not an economic act. That is, so soon as we concede, as is universally the case, what was just now discussed, namely, that the immediate consumption of wild fruits is not an.economic procedure, and therefore the fruits themselves have no economic value (except in so far as they save the production of economic values), then the consumption of values properly economic is no longer economic, for the act of consumption, in this last case, is not to be distinguished absolutely from that in the first case. Whether the fruit which one eats has been found accidentally, or stolen or bought, makes not the slightest difference in the act of eating itself, and in its direct consequences for the eater. Between desire and consumption lies the economic realm in unnumbered

interrelationships. Now, economic activity appears to be an equalization of sacrifices and gains (of forces or objects), a mere form in the sense that it presupposes values as its content, in order to be able to draw them into the equalizing movement.

But this appearance is not invincible. It will rather appear that the same process which constructs into an industrial system the values given as presuppositions itself produces the economic values.

To see this we need only remind ourselves in principle of the fact that the object is for us not a thing of value, so long as it is dissolved in the subjective process as an immediate stimulator of feelings, and thus at the same time is a self-evident competence of our sensibility. The object must first be detached from this sensibility, in order to acquire for our understanding the peculiar significance which we call value. For it is not only sure that desire, in and of itself, can never establish a value if it does not encounter obstacles. But if every desire could find its satisfaction without struggle and without diminution, an economic exchange of values would never come into existence. Indeed, desire itself would never have arisen to any considerable height if it could satisfy itself thus. It is only the postponement of the satisfaction through obstacles, the anxiety lest the object may escape, the tension of struggle for it, which brings into existence that aggregate of desire elements which may be designated as intensity or passion of volition. If, however, even the highest energy of desire were generated wholly from within, yet we would not accord value to the object which satisfies the desire if it came to us in unlimited abundance. The important thing, in that case, would be the total enjoyment, the existence of which guarantees to us the satisfaction of our wishes, but not that particular quantum of which we actually take possession, because this could be replaced quite as easily by another. Our consciousness would in this case simply be filled with the rhythm of the subjective desires and satisfactions, without attaching any significance to the object mediating the satisfaction. The desire, therefore, which on its part came into existence only through an absence of feelings of satisfaction, a condition of want or limitation, is the psychological expression of the distance between subject and object, in which the latter is represented as of value.

This distance necessary to the consequence in question is produced in certain cases by exchange, sacrifice, abstinence from objects; that is, in a word, the foregoing of feelings of satisfaction. This takes place, now, in the form of traffic co-temporaneous between two actors, each of whom requires of the other the abstinence in question as condition of the feeling of satisfaction. The feeling of satisfaction, as must be repeatedly emphasized, would not place itself in antithesis with its object as a value in our consciousness if the value were always near to us, so that we should have no occasion to separate the object from that consequence in us which is alone interesting. Through exchange, that is, through the economic system, there arise at the same time the values of industry, because exchange is the vehicle or producer of the distance between the subject and the object which transmutes the subjective state of feeling into objective valuation. Kant once summarized his Theory of Knowledge in the proposition: "The conditions of experience are at the same time the conditions of the objects of experience." By this he meant that the process which we call experience and the conceptions which constitute its contents or objects are subject to the selfsame laws of the reason. The objects can come into our experience, that is, be experienced by us, because they are conceptions in us; and the same energy which makes and defines the experience has also manifested itself in the structure of the objects. In the same sense we may say here: the possibility of the economic system is, at the same time, the possibility of economic objects. The very procedure between two possessors of objects (substances, labor-powers, rights, exchangeabilities of any sort), which procedure brings them into the so-called economic relationship, namely, reciprocal dedication, at the same time raises each of these objects into the category of values.

The difficulty which threatens from the side of logic, namely, that the values must first exist, and exist as values, in order to enter into the form and movement of industry, is now obviated, and by means of the perceived significance of that psychical relationship which we designated as the distance between us and the thing; for this differentiates the original subjective state of feeling into, first, the desiring subject anticipating the feelings; and, second, the object in antithesis with the subject, and containing in itself the value; while the distance, on its side, is produced by exchange, that is, by the two-sided operation of limitations, restriction, abstinence. The values of industry emerge, therefore, in the same reciprocity and relativity in which the economic character of values consists.

This transference of the idea of economic value from the character of isolating substantiality into the living process of relation may be further explained on the ground of those factors which we are accustomed to regard as the constituents of value, namely, availability and rarity. Availability appears here as the first condition, based upon the constitution of the industrial actor, under which alone an object can under any circumstances come into question. in economics. At the same time it is the presupposition of economic activity. In order that the value may reach a given degree, rarity must be associated with

availability, as a characteristic of the objects themselves. If we wish to fix economic values through demand and supply, demand would correspond with availability, supply with rarity. For the availability would decide whether we demand the object at all, the rarity the price which we are compelled to pay. The avail.

ability serves as the absolute constituent of the economic -- as that the extent of which must be determined in order that it may come into the course of economic exchange. We must from the beginning concede rarity as a merely relative element, since it means exclusively the quantitative relation in which the object in question stands to the existing aggregate of its kind; the qualitative nature of the object is not touched by its rarity.

The availability, however, seems to exist before all economic action, all comparison, all relation with other objects, and as the substantial factor of economic activity, whose movements are dependent upon itself.

The circumstance whose efficacy is herewith outlined is not correctly designated by the notion of utility or serviceableness.

What we mean in reality is the fact that the object is desired.

Al availability is, therefore, not in a situation to occasion economic operations with the object possessing the quality, if the availability does not at the same time have as a consequence that the objects are desired. As a matter of fact, this does not always occur. Any wish whatever may accord with any coNception of things useful to us; actual desire, however, which has economic significance and which sets our acts in motion, is not present in such wishes in case long poverty, constitutional laziness, diversion into other regions of interest, indifference of feeling toward the theoretically recognized utility, perceived impossibility of attaining the desired object, and other positive and negative elements work in the contrary direction. On the other hand, many sorts of things are desired by us, and also economically valued, which we cannot designate as useful or available without arbitrary distortion of verbal usage. Since, however, not everything that is available is also desired, if we decide to subsume everything. that is economically desired under the concept of "availability", it is logically demanded that we shall make the fact of being desired the definitively decisive element for economic movement. Even with this correction the criterion is not absolute, totally separable from the relativity of valuation. In the first place, as we saw above, the desire itself does not come to conscious definiteness unless obstacles, difficulties, interpose themselves between the object and the subject. We do not desire actually until enjoyment of the object measures itself upon intermediaries, where at least the price of patience, of resignment of other exertion or enjoyment, places at a distance from us the object to conquer which is the essence of desire for it. Its economic value now, second, which rises upon the basis of its being desired, can consist only in heightening or sublimating of that relativity which resides in desire. For the desired object does not pass into practical value, that is, into value that enters into the industrial movement, until its desirability is compared with that of another object, and thereby acquires a measure. Only when a second object is present, with reference to which I am sure that I am willing to give it for the first object, or vice versa, has each of the two an assignable economic value. The mere desire for an object does not lead to this valuation, since it finds in itself alone no measure. Only the comparison of desires, that is, the exchangeability of their objects, fixes each of the same as a value defined in accordance with its scale, that is, an economic value. The intensity of the individual desire, in and of itself, need not have a cumulative effect upon the economic value of the object, for since the latter comes to expression only in exchange, desire can determine it only in so far as it modifies the exchange. If now I desire an object very intensely, its exchange value is not thereby determined; for either I have the object not yet in my possession; in which case my desire, if I do not manifest it, can exert no influence upon the demand of the present possessor; he will rather adjust his claims according to the measure of his own interest in the object, or in accordance with his suppositions with reference to average interest; or, I have the object in my possession; in which case my terms will be either so high that the object is entirely excluded from exchange, in which instance it is to that extent no longer an economic value, or my demands must fall to the measure of the interest which a calculating person takes in the object. The decisive factor is this: that the economic, practically effective value is never a value in the abstract, but rather in its essence and idea a determined quantum of value; that this quantity in general can come into existence only through measurements of two intensities of desire against each other; that the form in which this measurement takes place within the industrial system is that of reciprocal gain and sacrifice; that consequently the economic object does not, as superficially appears, possess in its desirability an absolute element of value, but rather that this fact of being desired operates to give the object a value exclusively as being the foundation or the material of an actual or putative exchange.

Even in case we derive the valuation of objects from an absolute motive, namely, the labor expended upon them, and even if we assert that the value of goods is in inverse ratio to the productive capacity of the labor, yet we must still recognize the determination of the value of the objects as purely reciprocal, instead of a derivative from a single absolute standard. This being admitted, there arises the following relationship: A pair of boots has at a given time the same value as twenty meters of shirting. If now, through a new arrangement, the total labor demanded for the boots falls to one-half, they are worth only ten meters of shirting. Suppose now the labor time demanded for shirting is reduced one-half by improved machinery; the boots will then once more be the equivalent to twenty meters of shirting. If, again, the corresponding improvement affects all the laborers, and no goods are introduced which affect the relations between them, the two articles remain unchanged in their value as expressed in terms of each other. The change in the productive power of labor has an influence upon the value of the products only when it affects isolated portions of the economic organism, but not when it affects the organism as a whole. However we may exert ourselves, therefore, to express the value of the object through an absolute quantitative symbol, however qualified, it remains still only the relation, in which the various wares participate in this vehicle of value, which determines the value of each. Even under that presupposition, it is for the value of the separate objects as individuals wholly irrelevant how much or how little labor is invested in them. Only in so far as it is a quantity of labor greater or less in comparison with the quantity of labor invested in another object does each of the two acquire an economically effective value. But for the same reason it is, on the other hand, also unwarranted to complain at absence of the necessary stability of value in the daily wage of labor -- by which expression it is implied that the average return of a day's labor is a value-unity. That accusation is founded on the fact that the labor day constantly increases in productivity and power in exchange. Assuming, however, for the moment that labor is the one creator of value, the value of the time-unit of labor for the purpose of exchange of related goods is always the same; although, absolutely considered, it has increased, and corresponds to a larger quantum of each separate product. Since the reciprocal relation of the goods has remained the same, the relation of the labor time to each is the same as to the others. It may, therefore, remain, for the purpose of reckoning their relative values, a constant term.

This relativity of value, in consequence of which the given things stimulating feeling and desire come to be values only in the reciprocity of the give-and-take process, appears to lead to the consequence that value is nothing but the price, and that between the two objects no differences of scale can exist.

Consequently, the frequent falling away of the two from each other would refute the theory. Against that undeniable fact of varying ratio our theory asserts, to be sure, that there would never have been such a thing as a value if the universal phenomenon which we call price had not emerged. That a thing is worth something in a purely economic sense means that it is worth something to me, that is, that I am ready to give something for it. What in the world can move us to go beyond that naive subjective enjoyment of the things themselves, and to credit to them that peculiar significance which we call their value? This certainly cannot come from their scarcity in and of itself, for if this existed simply as a fact, and were not in some way or other modifiable by us, we would regard it as a natural, and, on account of the defective differentiations, perhaps entirely unrecognized, quality of the external cosmos. For, since it could not be otherwise; it would receive no emphasis beyond its inherent qualities. This valuation arises only from the fact that something must be paid for things: the patience of waiting, the effort of search, the application of labor-power, the abstinence from things otherwise desirable. Without price, therefore --

price originally in this extensive sense -- value does not come into being. That of two objects the one is more valuable than the other comes to pass subjectively as well as objectively only where one agent is ready to give this for that, but conversely that is not to be obtained for this. In transactions that have not become complicated the higher or lower value can be only the consequence or the expression of this immediate practical will to exchange. And if we say we exchange the things for each other because they are equally valuable, it is only that frequent inversion of thought and speech by which we also say that things pleased us because they were beautiful, whereas, in reality, they are beautiful because they please us.

If, thus, value is at the same time the offspring of price, it seems to be an identical proposition that their height must be the same. I refer now to the above proof, that in each individual case no contracting party pays the price which is to him, under the given circumstances, too high for the thing obtained. If in the poem of Chamisso the highwayman at the point of the pistol compels the victim to sell him his watch and rings for three coppers, the fact is that under the circumstances, since the victim could not otherwise save his life, the thing obtained in exchange was actually worth the price. No laborer would work for starvation wages if, in the situation in which he actually found himself, he did not prefer this wage to not working. The appearance of paradox in the assertion of the equivalence of value and price in every individual case arises only from the fact that certain conceptions of other kinds of equivalence of value and price are brought into our estimate of the case. The relative stability of the relationships by which the majority of exchanges are determined; on the other hand the analogies which fix still uncertain value-relations according to the norm of others already existing, produce the conceptions: if for a definite object this and that other definite object were exchange equivalents, these two or this group of objects would have equality in the scale of value; and if abnormal circumstances caused us to exchange the one object for values higher or lower in the scale, price and value would fall away from each other, although in each individual case, as a matter of fact, under consideration of its circumstances, they would coincide. We should not forget that the objective and just equivalence of value and price which we make the norm of the actual and the specific works only under very definite historical and technical conditions; and, with change of these conditions, at once vanishes. Between the norm itself and the cases which are characterized as exceptional or as adequate no general difference exists, but, so to speak, only a numerical difference -- somewhat as we say of an extraordinarily eminent or degraded individual,

"He is really no longer a man." The fact is that this idea of man is only an average; it would lose its normative character at the moment in which the majority of men ascended or descended to that grade, which then would pass for the generically human.

In order to reach this perception we must, to be sure, extricate ourselves from deep-rooted conceptions of value, which also have an assured practical justification. These conceptions, in the case of relationships that are somewhat complex, rest in two strata with reference to each other. The one is formed from the traditions of society, from the majority of experiences, from demands that seem to be purely logical; the other, from individual correlations, from the demands of the moment, from the constraint of given facts. In contrast with the rapid changes within this latter stratum, the gradual evolution of the former and its construction out of elaboration of our perceptions is lost to sight, and the former appears as alone justified as the expression of an objective ratio. Where now, in case of an exchange under the given circumstances, the valuations of sacrifice and gain at least balance each other -- for otherwise no agent would consummate the exchange -- yet judged by those general criteria a discrepancy appears, in such a case we speak of a divergence between value and price. This occurs most decisively under the two presuppositions (almost always united), viz., first, that a single value-quality passes as economic value in general, and two objects consequently can be recognized as equal in value, only in so far as the like quantum of that fundamental value is present in them; and, second, that a definite proportion between two values appears as a something that must be, with the emphasis of a not merely objective, but also a moral demand. The conception, for example, that the essential value-element in all values is the labor time objectified in them is utilized in both these assumptions, and thus gives a direct or an indirect standard which fixes the value independent of price, and makes the latter vibrate in changing plus and minus differences, as compared with the former. Now it is evident, to be sure, that if we from the start recognize only a single value-substance, only that price corresponds to the value so contained which contains precisely an equivalent amount of that same value. According to this principle the value should be the first and fixed element; the price should constitute a more or less adequate secondary element. But this consequence, supposing everything else is conceded, does not in fact follow.

The fact of that single measure of value leaves entirely unexplained how labor-power comes to have value. It would hardly have occurred if the labor-power had not, by acting upon various materials and by creating various products, made the possibility of exchange; or unless the exercise of the power had been recognized as a sacrifice made for the gain of the object achieved by the sacrifice. Thus labor-power also comes into the value-category through the possibility and reality of exchange, quite unaffected by the circumstance that later labor-power may itself furnish a measure, within the value-category, for the other contents. If the labor-power is thus also the content of that value, it receives its form as value only through the fact that it enters into the relation of sacrifice and gain, or price and value (here in the narrower sense). In the cases of discrepancy between price and value, the one contracting party would, according to this theory, give a quantum of immediately realizable labor-power for a lesser quantum of the same. Yet other circumstances, not containing labor-power, are in such wise connected with this case that the party still completes the exchange; for example: the satisfaction of an economic need, amateurish fancy, fraud, monopoly, and similar circumstances. In the wider and subjective sense, therefore, the equivalence of value and counter-value remains in these cases, while the simple norm, labor-power, which makes the discrepancy possible, does not on its side cease to derive its genesis as a vehicle of value from exchange.

The qualitative determination of objects, which subjectively signifies their desirability, can consequently not maintain the claim of constituting an absolute value-magnitude. It is always the relation of the desires to each other, realized in exchange, which makes their objects economic values. This determination appears more immediately in connection with the other element supposed to constitute value, namely, scarcity, or relative rarity. Exchange is, indeed, nothing else than the

inter-individual attempt to improve conditions rising out of scarcity of goods; that is, to reduce as far as possible the amount of subjective abstinence by the mode of distributing the given stock. Thereupon follows immediately a universal correlation between that which we call scarcity-value and that which we call exchange-value, a correlation which appears, for instance, in the relation of socialism to both. We may, perhaps, indicate the economic purposes of socialism comprehensively and abstractly in this way, namely, that it strives to abolish scarcity-value; that is, that modification of the value of things which arises from their rarity or abundance; for it is abundance which reduces the value of labor. There should be less labor, in order that labor may be appraised according to the quality-value, without depression on account of the quantity. On the other hand, the means of enjoyment should lose that value which they now have on account of their restricted quantity; that is, they should be accessible to all. Accordingly, Marx held that in the capitalistic type of society, that is, the sort of society which socialism wishes to abolish, exchange-value alone is decisive, while use-value no longer plays any role. While socialism despises exchange-value quite as much as scarcity-value, it calls attention to the radical connection between the two.

For us, however, the connection is more important in the reverse direction. I have already emphasized the fact that scarcity of goods would scarcely have a valuation of them as a consequence if it were not modifiable by us. It is, however, modifiable in two ways: either through devotion of labor-power, which increases the stock of the goods in question, or through devotion of already possessed objects, which as substitutes abolish the rarity of the most desired objects for the individual. Accordingly, we may say immediately that the scarcity of goods in proportion to the desires centering upon them objectively determines exchange; that, however, the exchange on its side brings scarcity into force as an element of value. It is a thoroughgoing mistake of theories of value to assume that, when utility and rarity are given, economic value -- that is, exchange movement -- is something to be taken for granted, a conceptually necessary consequence of those premises. In this they are by no means correct. In case, for instance, there were alongside of these presuppositions an ascetic renunciation, or if they only instigated to conflict or robbery -- which is, to be sure, often enough the case -- no economic value and no economic life would emerge. Exchange is a sociological structure sui generis, a primary form and function of inter-individual life, which by no means emerges as a logical consequence from those qualitative and quantitative properties of things which we call availability and rarity. On the contrary, it is rather the case that these two properties derive their value-creating significance only under the presupposition of exchange. Where exchange, the offering of a sacrifice for the purpose of a gain, is for any reason excluded, there no rarity of the desired object can confer upon it economic value until the possibility of that relation reappears. We may express the relation in this way: The significance of the object for the individual always rests merely in its desirability; so far as that is concerned which the object is to do for us, its qualitative character is decisive, and when we have it, it is a matter of indifference in this respect whether there exist besides many, few, or no specimens of the same sort. (I do not treat here especially the cases in which rarity itself is a species of qualitative character, which makes the object desirable to us, as in the case of old postage stamps, curiosities, antiquities without aesthetic or historical value, etc. I also disregard. other cases, interesting in themselves, here however in principle insignificant, namely, those psychological subsidiary phenomena which frequently arise from scarcity itself, where they have no effect upon acquisition of the object.) The enjoyment of things, therefore, so soon as possession of them is achieved, the positive practical significance of their actuality for us, is quite independent of the scarcity question, since this affects only a numerical relation to things, which we do not have, to be sure, but which, according to the hypothesis, we do not desire to have. The only question in point with reference to things, apart from enjoyment of them, is the way to them. So soon as this way is a long and difficult one, leading over sacrifice in the shape of strain of the patience, disappointment, labor, self-denial, etc., we call the object scarce. Paradoxical as it is, things are not difficult to obtain because they are scarce, but they are scarce because they are difficult to obtain. The inflexible external fact that there is a deficient stock of certain goods to satisfy all our desires for them would be in itself insignificant. Whether they are scarce in the sense of economic value is decided simply by the circumstance of the measure of energy, patience, devotion to acquisition, which is necessary in order to obtain them. Let us suppose a stock of goods which suffices to cover all the demands centered upon it, but which is so disposed that every portion of it is to be obtained only with considerable effort and sacrifice.

Then the result for its valuation and its practical significance would be precisely the same which, under the presupposition of equal availability, we have been accustomed to derive from its scarcity. The difficulty of attainment, that is, the magnitude of the sacrifice involved in exchange, is thus the element that peculiarly constitutes value. Scarcity constitutes only the external appearance of this element, only the externalizing of it in the form of quantity. We fail

to observe that scarcity, purely as such, is only a negative property, an existence characterized by a non-existence. The non-existent, however, cannot be operative. Every positive consequence must proceed from a positive property and force, of which that negative property is only the shadow. These concrete energies are, however, manifestly only those that are put into action in the exchange, so that the increase of value starts from that increasing magnitude whose negative is the scarcity of the object.

Finally, by way of corollary, I will add a more conceptual deduction, namely, that the usual conception of the scarcity theory must presuppose the value which it tries to derive from scarcity. According to this conception, an object of economic desire acquires value if no unlimited number of specimens of its kind is at hand; that is, if the present quantity of such objects does not cover a series of needs that look to it for

satisfaction. The failure of these needs to be covered is felt as a painful condition which ought not to be, as the negation of value. The covering of these needs must be something having value. Otherwise the failure could exert no such effect. If, however, this defect is necessary to establish the value of the present quantity, the value is thereby presupposed whose establishment is in question. The existing quantity has value because the lacking quantity has value. Otherwise its lack could never establish a value. Let us suppose the quantity A, which would completely cover the need, to be divided into two parts: first, the portion actually present, M, and, second, the merely ideally present, N. According to the theory, the value M is determined by the fact that N is not present. N must, as we said, have a value in order to produce this consequence. In order that it may have this value, we must, however, think it as present, and, on the contrary, M as not present. Otherwise the whole of A would be accessible, and therefore, according to the scarcity theory,

no portion of it would have a value. The value of the actual quantity is based on that of the non-existing quantity, that of the non-existing quantity (which I must think in this connection as present) on that of the existing quantity (which I must think as non-existent). The scarcity element is thus to be accounted for only relatively, equally with that element which has its source in the significance of the object for the feelings. As little as the fact of being desired can scarcity create for the object a valuation otherwise than in the reciprocal relation with another object existing under like conditions. We may examine the one object ever so closely with reference to its self-sufficient properties, we shall never find the economic value; since this consists exclusively in the reciprocal relationship, which comes into being between several objects on the basis of these properties, each determining the other, and each giving to the other the significance which each in turn receives from the other.